100 DAYS OF CULTIVATING DEEP ROOTS OF GRATITUDE

MORE THAN
GRATITUDE

THROUGH GUIDED JOURNALING, PRAYER, & SCRIPTURE

THIS BOOK BELONGS TO :

_____

_____

_____

_____

KORIE HEROLD | paige tate & co.

Also by Korie Herold

As You Grow : A Modern Memory Book for Baby
As We Grow : A Modern Memory Book for Married Couples
Our Christmas Story : A Modern Christmas Memory Book
Growing You : A Keepsake Pregnancy Journal
Growing Up : A Modern Memory Book for the School Years
Around Our Table : A Modern Heirloom Recipe Book

More Than Gratitude : 100 Days of Cultivating Deep Roots of
Gratitude through Guided Journaling, Prayer, and Scripture
Copyright © Korie Herold
Published in 2021 by Blue Star Press
Paige Tate & Co. is an imprint of Blue Star Press
PO Box 8835, Bend, OR 97708
contact@paigetate.com | www.paigetate.com

Illustrations and Design by Korie Herold

ISBN: 9781950968497
Printed in China
10 9 8 7 6 5 4 3 2 1

This journal is dedicated to the intentional ones, those who know that what we do with the time we're given is of the utmost importance.

May you cling to the truth in your walk daily.

INTRODUCTION | *The Heart of this Journal*

How we experience the world is based on so many factors: where we live, how we spend our time, who we surround ourselves with, and what choices we make for ourselves along the way. With so many things demanding our attention, it can be easy to feel overwhelmed and fall victim to the hardships of our world. But when we're faced with those hardships, we always have the choice to see the good, knowing this world is not our home. We have the option to choose hope over fear, positivity over pessimism, and abundance over scarcity. In other words, we have the choice to view our challenges as opportunities to grow and to be changed.

I created this gratitude journal because it's the tool I always wished I had for my own personal daily reflections, self-growth, and walk with the Lord. It's a simple and beautiful place to meditate on my days—a journal that invites me in, yet isn't overwhelming to write in. It's a place to be intentional about my time and my heart.

This isn't just another gratitude journal, because I think there's more involved in growing deep roots of gratitude than quickly acknowledging a couple things you're thankful for each day. There's nothing wrong with that style of journal, but that's not what this one is for. This journal touches on gratitude, kindness, forgiveness, growth, and prayer each day you choose to use it, so those thoughts linger with you day in and day out. It leaves you consistently seeking good in your situation and encourages upward growth. Consider this journal a tool to help you get from point A to point B in the season of your life you choose to use this by doing the personal heart work this journal brings forward.

I think there is something powerful about the written word that cannot be underestimated. Taking quiet time to sit, reflect, and write by hand about our days gives us a chance to process our feelings, make sense of our experiences, and gain new perspectives on this precious life He has given us. For me, journaling is a gift because it gives me something to revisit whenever I want to remember what I was feeling or thinking during a particular season of my life. It's incredibly special to preserve those memories and life lessons so that I can appreciate them for years to come. I have a feeling you feel the same way if you're reading this. Journaling by hand also provides a tangible experience that you just can't get typing away on your computer or phone. Cherish this as an opportunity to slow down, honor your thoughts, and store them on these pages that you can hold in your hands and carry with you along the way.

Learning to lead a life of abundance—one where we embrace our days with a whole-hearted "yes and!"—is the exact reason I created this journal. The writing prompts I selected for each day are the heart of this book and ones that I hope will offer you comfort and courage for personal growth and reflection. Each prompt is an area of life I find important to check in on daily, and I paired each below with a scripture as to why it was chosen for the journal. Take a minute to dive into your Bible and look up each one listed below:

    1. Gratitude - It's important to start here first each day. This prompt guides our hearts to see the good in each day we are given. No matter how hard the day might have been, something good can always be found. (See 1 Thessalonians 5:18)

    2. Kindness - This prompt encourages us to find ways to spread kindness to those around us each day, in ways big or small. (See Luke 6:35)

    3. Forgiveness/Letting Go - This prompt helps us to not dwell on things we can't change, and find the strength to move on. Physically writing this one down is important in the process of letting go over time. (See Ephesians 4:32)

4. _Mindfulness/Growth_ - This prompt gives us space to document and relish in what we're learning as a child of God. It can be anything on your heart. Literally anything. (See Proverbs 1:7)

5. _Prayer_ - This prompt connects you with Our Heavenly Father and allows you to witness your own answered prayers over time through the use of this journal and reading back on past entries. (See 1 John 5:14)

6. _Highlights_ - Consider this one a bonus. It's a place to document a brief history of your daily life as it unfolds alongside your growth journey within these pages. It's a way to help jog your memory during this season of reflection and intentionality.

The entries are short and sweet, making them easy to complete at the end of each day as a form of self-care and thanksgiving. By the end of 100 days, it's my hope that you are able to look back on what you've written and contemplate the ways you've grown during your time of using this journal. And, if you miss a day, that's okay too. Don't feel any pressure or failure if you don't find quiet time to sit and write every single day. The fact that you are showing up for yourself at all in this way deserves praise.

Read that last part again.

The fact that you are showing up for yourself at all in this way deserves praise.

The words of scripture found at the start of each entry were collected from people who have shown up for me along the way. These individuals come from all different walks of life and have been a part of my own journey of faith and growth. It was important to me to gather the verses that have motivated, encouraged, and moved them, and share them here with you. Doing so felt like a gentle way to remind us all that we are not alone in this journey through life. The importance of community cannot be understated, and a valuable part of any gratitude practice is taking time to cherish the people who lift you up and make you feel whole.

After you've written your thoughts for the day, I encourage you to linger for a little while longer on each daily scripture found at the top of each page. Pull out your Bible, look them up, and read them in context. You'll get even more out of the use of this journal by diving deeper into the verses provided. The verses included in this journal cover a wide array of topics, and I pray they serve as a jumping off point for your own personal studies in the Word during this season.

I'll end with this: It is my biggest hope that this journal becomes a valuable tool for you as you navigate your way through this season, no matter what it may look like for you.

Here's to always looking for the light, and being a light that shines on those around us.

Onward & Upward!
Korie Herold

I would love to see how you incorporate _More Than Gratitude_ into your routine. Use #MoreThanGratitude and tag @korieherold to connect on social media.

DAY ONE | *Before You Begin*

As you look ahead to these next 100 days, take a moment to write down where you are currently at in your life. You'll be revisiting this later. Reflect on your joys, your struggles, your cares, or your concerns right now. Maybe you are starting a new chapter, a new job, or a new relationship. Maybe you're grieving the loss of a loved one. Maybe you're feeling a bit apathetic about life and need a spark. If someone were to ask you, "How are you? No really, *how are you?*", what would you say? That's what you should pen here. Being honest with yourself isn't always easy, but it is a gift that pays dividends in the long run.

This is your starting point.

Go.

*See, I am doing a new thing! ... I am making a way
in the wilderness and streams in the wasteland.*
Isaiah 43:19

TODAY I AM GRATEFUL FOR :

KINDNESS I SHARED TODAY :

I NEED TO LET GO OF THIS :

I LEARNED THIS TODAY :

A PRAYER ON MY HEART TODAY :

MY HIGHLIGHTS OF THE DAY :

*Consider it pure joy ... whenever you face trials of many kinds, because
you know that the testing of your faith produces perseverance.*
James 1:2-3

TODAY I AM GRATEFUL FOR : _____

_____

_____

_____

_____

KINDNESS I SHARED TODAY : _____

_____

_____

_____

_____

I NEED TO LET GO OF THIS : _____

_____

_____

_____

_____

I LEARNED THIS TODAY : _____

_____

_____

_____

_____

A PRAYER ON MY HEART TODAY : _____

_____

_____

_____

_____

MY HIGHLIGHTS OF THE DAY : _____

_____

_____

_____

_____

_____

Blessed are the peacemakers, for they will be called children of God.
Matthew 5:9

TODAY I AM GRATEFUL FOR : _____

_____

_____

_____

_____

KINDNESS I SHARED TODAY : _____

_____

_____

_____

_____

I NEED TO LET GO OF THIS : _____

_____

_____

_____

_____

I LEARNED THIS TODAY : _____

_____

_____

_____

_____

A PRAYER ON MY HEART TODAY : _____

_____

_____

_____

MY HIGHLIGHTS OF THE DAY : _____

_____

_____

_____

_____

'Love your neighbor as yourself.'
Matthew 22:39

TODAY I AM GRATEFUL FOR : _____

_____

_____

_____

_____

KINDNESS I SHARED TODAY : _____

_____

_____

_____

_____

I NEED TO LET GO OF THIS : _____

_____

_____

_____

_____

I LEARNED THIS TODAY : _____

_____

_____

_____

_____

A PRAYER ON MY HEART TODAY : _____

_____

_____

_____

_____

MY HIGHLIGHTS OF THE DAY : _____

_____

_____

_____

_____

_____

In peace I will lie down and sleep, for you alone,
Lord, make me dwell in safety.
Psalm 4:8

TODAY I AM GRATEFUL FOR : _____

_____

_____

_____

_____

KINDNESS I SHARED TODAY : _____

_____

_____

_____

_____

I NEED TO LET GO OF THIS : _____

_____

_____

_____

_____

I LEARNED THIS TODAY : _____

_____

_____

_____

_____

A PRAYER ON MY HEART TODAY : _____

_____

_____

_____

_____

MY HIGHLIGHTS OF THE DAY : _____

_____

_____

_____

_____

_____

He will cover you with his feathers, and under his wings you will
find refuge; his faithfulness will be your shield and rampart.
Psalm 91:4

TODAY I AM GRATEFUL FOR : _____
_____
_____
_____
_____

KINDNESS I SHARED TODAY : _____
_____
_____
_____
_____

I NEED TO LET GO OF THIS : _____
_____
_____
_____
_____

I LEARNED THIS TODAY : _____
_____
_____
_____
_____

A PRAYER ON MY HEART TODAY : _____
_____
_____
_____

MY HIGHLIGHTS OF THE DAY : _____
_____
_____
_____
_____
_____

Carry each other's burdens, and in this way you will fulfill the law of Christ.
Galatians 6:2

TODAY I AM GRATEFUL FOR : _____

KINDNESS I SHARED TODAY : _____

I NEED TO LET GO OF THIS : _____

I LEARNED THIS TODAY : _____

A PRAYER ON MY HEART TODAY : _____

MY HIGHLIGHTS OF THE DAY : _____

Anxiety weighs down the heart, but a kind word cheers it up.
Proverbs 12:25

TODAY I AM GRATEFUL FOR : _____

_____

_____

_____

_____

KINDNESS I SHARED TODAY : _____

_____

_____

_____

_____

I NEED TO LET GO OF THIS : _____

_____

_____

_____

_____

I LEARNED THIS TODAY : _____

_____

_____

_____

_____

A PRAYER ON MY HEART TODAY : _____

_____

_____

_____

MY HIGHLIGHTS OF THE DAY : _____

_____

_____

_____

_____

Do not conform to the pattern of this world,
but be transformed by the renewing of your mind.
Romans 12:2

TODAY I AM GRATEFUL FOR : _____

_____

_____

_____

KINDNESS I SHARED TODAY : _____

_____

_____

_____

I NEED TO LET GO OF THIS : _____

_____

_____

_____

I LEARNED THIS TODAY : _____

_____

_____

_____

A PRAYER ON MY HEART TODAY : _____

_____

_____

MY HIGHLIGHTS OF THE DAY : _____

_____

_____

_____

Then you will know the truth, and the truth will set you free.
John 8:32

TODAY I AM GRATEFUL FOR : _____
_____
_____
_____
_____

KINDNESS I SHARED TODAY : _____
_____
_____
_____
_____

I NEED TO LET GO OF THIS : _____
_____
_____
_____
_____

I LEARNED THIS TODAY : _____
_____
_____
_____
_____

A PRAYER ON MY HEART TODAY : _____
_____
_____
_____

MY HIGHLIGHTS OF THE DAY : _____
_____
_____
_____
_____
_____

But I tell you, love your enemies and pray for those who persecute you.
Matthew 5:44

TODAY I AM GRATEFUL FOR : _____

_____

_____

_____

_____

KINDNESS I SHARED TODAY : _____

_____

_____

_____

_____

I NEED TO LET GO OF THIS : _____

_____

_____

_____

_____

I LEARNED THIS TODAY : _____

_____

_____

_____

A PRAYER ON MY HEART TODAY : _____

_____

_____

_____

MY HIGHLIGHTS OF THE DAY : _____

_____

_____

_____

_____

God is our refuge and strength, an ever-present help in trouble.
Psalm 46:1

TODAY I AM GRATEFUL FOR : _____

_____

_____

_____

_____

KINDNESS I SHARED TODAY : _____

_____

_____

_____

_____

I NEED TO LET GO OF THIS : _____

_____

_____

_____

_____

I LEARNED THIS TODAY : _____

_____

_____

_____

_____

A PRAYER ON MY HEART TODAY : _____

_____

_____

_____

_____

MY HIGHLIGHTS OF THE DAY : _____

_____

_____

_____

_____

_____

_____

*Now to him who is able to do immeasurably more than all we
ask or imagine, according to his power that is at work within us.*
Ephesians 3:20

TODAY I AM GRATEFUL FOR : _____

_____

_____

_____

_____

KINDNESS I SHARED TODAY : _____

_____

_____

_____

_____

I NEED TO LET GO OF THIS : _____

_____

_____

_____

_____

I LEARNED THIS TODAY : _____

_____

_____

_____

_____

A PRAYER ON MY HEART TODAY : _____

_____

_____

_____

MY HIGHLIGHTS OF THE DAY : _____

_____

_____

_____

_____

_____

And we know that in all things God works for the good of those
who love him, who have been called according to his purpose.
Romans 8:28

TODAY I AM GRATEFUL FOR : _____

_____

_____

_____

_____

KINDNESS I SHARED TODAY : _____

_____

_____

_____

_____

I NEED TO LET GO OF THIS : _____

_____

_____

_____

_____

I LEARNED THIS TODAY : _____

_____

_____

_____

_____

A PRAYER ON MY HEART TODAY : _____

_____

_____

_____

MY HIGHLIGHTS OF THE DAY : _____

_____

_____

_____

_____

*Love one another ... By this everyone will know that
you are my disciples, if you love one another.
John 13:34-35*

TODAY I AM GRATEFUL FOR : _____

_____

_____

_____

_____

KINDNESS I SHARED TODAY : _____

_____

_____

_____

_____

I NEED TO LET GO OF THIS : _____

_____

_____

_____

_____

I LEARNED THIS TODAY : _____

_____

_____

_____

_____

A PRAYER ON MY HEART TODAY : _____

_____

_____

_____

_____

MY HIGHLIGHTS OF THE DAY : _____

_____

_____

_____

_____

Blessed are the merciful, for they will be shown mercy.
Matthew 5:7

TODAY I AM GRATEFUL FOR : _____

_____

_____

_____

_____

KINDNESS I SHARED TODAY : _____

_____

_____

_____

_____

I NEED TO LET GO OF THIS : _____

_____

_____

_____

_____

I LEARNED THIS TODAY : _____

_____

_____

_____

_____

A PRAYER ON MY HEART TODAY : _____

_____

_____

_____

_____

MY HIGHLIGHTS OF THE DAY : _____

_____

_____

_____

_____

_____

My people will live in peaceful dwelling places,
in secure homes, in undisturbed places of rest.
Isaiah 32:18

TODAY I AM GRATEFUL FOR : _____

_____

_____

_____

_____

KINDNESS I SHARED TODAY : _____

_____

_____

_____

_____

I NEED TO LET GO OF THIS : _____

_____

_____

_____

_____

I LEARNED THIS TODAY : _____

_____

_____

_____

A PRAYER ON MY HEART TODAY : _____

_____

_____

_____

MY HIGHLIGHTS OF THE DAY : _____

_____

_____

_____

_____

The peace of God, which transcends all understanding,
will guard your hearts and your minds in Christ Jesus.
Philippians 4:7

TODAY I AM GRATEFUL FOR :

KINDNESS I SHARED TODAY :

I NEED TO LET GO OF THIS :

I LEARNED THIS TODAY :

A PRAYER ON MY HEART TODAY :

MY HIGHLIGHTS OF THE DAY :

Be on your guard; stand firm in the faith; be courageous; be strong.
1 Corinthians 16:13

TODAY I AM GRATEFUL FOR : _____

_____

_____

_____

_____

KINDNESS I SHARED TODAY : _____

_____

_____

_____

_____

I NEED TO LET GO OF THIS : _____

_____

_____

_____

_____

I LEARNED THIS TODAY : _____

_____

_____

_____

_____

A PRAYER ON MY HEART TODAY : _____

_____

_____

_____

MY HIGHLIGHTS OF THE DAY : _____

_____

_____

_____

_____

*Put on the full armor of God, so that you can
take your stand against the devil's schemes.
Ephesians 6:11*

TODAY I AM GRATEFUL FOR : _____

_____

_____

_____

_____

KINDNESS I SHARED TODAY : _____

_____

_____

_____

_____

I NEED TO LET GO OF THIS : _____

_____

_____

_____

_____

I LEARNED THIS TODAY : _____

_____

_____

_____

_____

A PRAYER ON MY HEART TODAY : _____

_____

_____

_____

_____

MY HIGHLIGHTS OF THE DAY : _____

_____

_____

_____

_____

Love the Lord your God with all your heart and
with all your soul and with all your mind.
Matthew 22:37

TODAY I AM GRATEFUL FOR : _____

_____

_____

_____

_____

KINDNESS I SHARED TODAY : _____

_____

_____

_____

_____

I NEED TO LET GO OF THIS : _____

_____

_____

_____

_____

I LEARNED THIS TODAY : _____

_____

_____

_____

_____

A PRAYER ON MY HEART TODAY : _____

_____

_____

_____

MY HIGHLIGHTS OF THE DAY : _____

_____

_____

_____

_____

In their hearts humans plan their course,
but the Lord establishes their steps.
Proverbs 16:9

TODAY I AM GRATEFUL FOR : _____

_____

_____

_____

_____

KINDNESS I SHARED TODAY : _____

_____

_____

_____

_____

I NEED TO LET GO OF THIS : _____

_____

_____

_____

_____

I LEARNED THIS TODAY : _____

_____

_____

_____

_____

A PRAYER ON MY HEART TODAY : _____

_____

_____

_____

MY HIGHLIGHTS OF THE DAY : _____

_____

_____

_____

_____

To act justly and to love mercy and to walk humbly with your God.
Micah 6:8

TODAY I AM GRATEFUL FOR : _____

_____

_____

_____

_____

KINDNESS I SHARED TODAY : _____

_____

_____

_____

_____

I NEED TO LET GO OF THIS : _____

_____

_____

_____

_____

I LEARNED THIS TODAY : _____

_____

_____

_____

_____

A PRAYER ON MY HEART TODAY : _____

_____

_____

_____

MY HIGHLIGHTS OF THE DAY : _____

_____

_____

_____

_____

_____

I have told you these things, so that in me you may have peace. In this world you will have trouble. But take heart! I have overcome the world.
John 16:33

TODAY I AM GRATEFUL FOR : _____

_____

_____

_____

_____

KINDNESS I SHARED TODAY : _____

_____

_____

_____

_____

I NEED TO LET GO OF THIS : _____

_____

_____

_____

_____

I LEARNED THIS TODAY : _____

_____

_____

_____

_____

A PRAYER ON MY HEART TODAY : _____

_____

_____

_____

MY HIGHLIGHTS OF THE DAY : _____

_____

_____

_____

_____

Rejoice in the Lord always. I will say it again: Rejoice!
Philippians 4:4

TODAY I AM GRATEFUL FOR : _____

_____

_____

_____

_____

KINDNESS I SHARED TODAY : _____

_____

_____

_____

_____

I NEED TO LET GO OF THIS : _____

_____

_____

_____

_____

I LEARNED THIS TODAY : _____

_____

_____

_____

_____

A PRAYER ON MY HEART TODAY : _____

_____

_____

_____

MY HIGHLIGHTS OF THE DAY : _____

_____

_____

_____

_____

You will keep in perfect peace those whose minds
are steadfast, because they trust in you.
Isaiah 26:3

TODAY I AM GRATEFUL FOR :

KINDNESS I SHARED TODAY :

I NEED TO LET GO OF THIS :

I LEARNED THIS TODAY :

A PRAYER ON MY HEART TODAY :

MY HIGHLIGHTS OF THE DAY :

As iron sharpens iron, so one person sharpens another.
Proverbs 27:17

TODAY I AM GRATEFUL FOR : _____

_____

_____

_____

_____

KINDNESS I SHARED TODAY : _____

_____

_____

_____

_____

I NEED TO LET GO OF THIS : _____

_____

_____

_____

_____

I LEARNED THIS TODAY : _____

_____

_____

_____

A PRAYER ON MY HEART TODAY : _____

_____

_____

_____

MY HIGHLIGHTS OF THE DAY : _____

_____

_____

_____

_____

*Lead a quiet life: You should mind your
own business and work with your hands.*
1 Thessalonians 4:11

TODAY I AM GRATEFUL FOR : _____

_____

_____

_____

KINDNESS I SHARED TODAY : _____

_____

_____

_____

I NEED TO LET GO OF THIS : _____

_____

_____

_____

I LEARNED THIS TODAY : _____

_____

_____

_____

A PRAYER ON MY HEART TODAY : _____

_____

_____

_____

MY HIGHLIGHTS OF THE DAY : _____

_____

_____

_____

_____

Take delight in the Lord, and he will give you the desires of your heart.
Psalm 37:4

TODAY I AM GRATEFUL FOR : _____

_____

_____

_____

_____

KINDNESS I SHARED TODAY : _____

_____

_____

_____

_____

I NEED TO LET GO OF THIS : _____

_____

_____

_____

_____

I LEARNED THIS TODAY : _____

_____

_____

_____

_____

A PRAYER ON MY HEART TODAY : _____

_____

_____

_____

MY HIGHLIGHTS OF THE DAY : _____

_____

_____

_____

_____

*When you ask, you must believe and not doubt, because the one who
doubts is like a wave of the sea, blown and tossed by the wind.*
James 1:6

TODAY I AM GRATEFUL FOR :

KINDNESS I SHARED TODAY :

I NEED TO LET GO OF THIS :

I LEARNED THIS TODAY :

A PRAYER ON MY HEART TODAY :

MY HIGHLIGHTS OF THE DAY :

I sought the Lord, and he answered me; he delivered me from all my fears.
Psalm 34:4

TODAY I AM GRATEFUL FOR :

KINDNESS I SHARED TODAY :

I NEED TO LET GO OF THIS :

I LEARNED THIS TODAY :

A PRAYER ON MY HEART TODAY :

MY HIGHLIGHTS OF THE DAY :

You, Lord, are my lamp; the Lord turns my darkness into light.
2 Samuel 22:29

TODAY I AM GRATEFUL FOR : _____

_____

_____

_____

_____

KINDNESS I SHARED TODAY : _____

_____

_____

_____

_____

I NEED TO LET GO OF THIS : _____

_____

_____

_____

_____

I LEARNED THIS TODAY : _____

_____

_____

_____

_____

A PRAYER ON MY HEART TODAY : _____

_____

_____

_____

_____

MY HIGHLIGHTS OF THE DAY : _____

_____

_____

_____

_____

_____

For you were once darkness, but now you are
light in the Lord. Live as children of light.
Ephesians 5:8

TODAY I AM GRATEFUL FOR : _____

_____

_____

_____

_____

KINDNESS I SHARED TODAY : _____

_____

_____

_____

_____

I NEED TO LET GO OF THIS : _____

_____

_____

_____

_____

I LEARNED THIS TODAY : _____

_____

_____

_____

_____

A PRAYER ON MY HEART TODAY : _____

_____

_____

_____

MY HIGHLIGHTS OF THE DAY : _____

_____

_____

_____

_____

_____

Dear children, let us not love with words
or speech but with actions and in truth.
1 John 3:18

TODAY I AM GRATEFUL FOR : _____

_____

_____

_____

_____

KINDNESS I SHARED TODAY : _____

_____

_____

_____

_____

I NEED TO LET GO OF THIS : _____

_____

_____

_____

_____

I LEARNED THIS TODAY : _____

_____

_____

_____

_____

A PRAYER ON MY HEART TODAY : _____

_____

_____

_____

_____

MY HIGHLIGHTS OF THE DAY : _____

_____

_____

_____

_____

Let us not become weary in doing good, for at the proper
time we will reap a harvest if we do not give up.
Galatians 6:9

TODAY I AM GRATEFUL FOR : _____

_____
_____
_____
_____

KINDNESS I SHARED TODAY : _____

_____
_____
_____
_____

I NEED TO LET GO OF THIS : _____

_____
_____
_____
_____

I LEARNED THIS TODAY : _____

_____
_____
_____
_____

A PRAYER ON MY HEART TODAY : _____

_____
_____
_____

MY HIGHLIGHTS OF THE DAY : _____

_____
_____
_____
_____

Who comforts us in all our troubles, so that we can comfort those
in any trouble with the comfort we ourselves receive from God.
2 Corinthians 1:4

TODAY I AM GRATEFUL FOR : _____

_____

_____

_____

_____

KINDNESS I SHARED TODAY : _____

_____

_____

_____

_____

I NEED TO LET GO OF THIS : _____

_____

_____

_____

_____

I LEARNED THIS TODAY : _____

_____

_____

_____

_____

A PRAYER ON MY HEART TODAY : _____

_____

_____

_____

_____

MY HIGHLIGHTS OF THE DAY : _____

_____

_____

_____

_____

_____

The Lord is my rock, my fortress and my deliverer.
Psalm 18:2

TODAY I AM GRATEFUL FOR : _____
_____
_____
_____
_____

KINDNESS I SHARED TODAY : _____
_____
_____
_____
_____

I NEED TO LET GO OF THIS : _____
_____
_____
_____
_____

I LEARNED THIS TODAY : _____
_____
_____
_____
_____

A PRAYER ON MY HEART TODAY : _____
_____
_____
_____
_____

MY HIGHLIGHTS OF THE DAY : _____
_____
_____
_____
_____

The whole earth is full of his glory.
Isaiah 6:3

TODAY I AM GRATEFUL FOR : _____

_____

_____

_____

_____

KINDNESS I SHARED TODAY : _____

_____

_____

_____

_____

I NEED TO LET GO OF THIS : _____

_____

_____

_____

_____

I LEARNED THIS TODAY : _____

_____

_____

_____

_____

A PRAYER ON MY HEART TODAY : _____

_____

_____

_____

_____

MY HIGHLIGHTS OF THE DAY : _____

_____

_____

_____

_____

Even though I walk through the darkest valley, I will fear no evil,
for you are with me; your rod and your staff, they comfort me.
Psalm 23:4

TODAY I AM GRATEFUL FOR :

KINDNESS I SHARED TODAY :

I NEED TO LET GO OF THIS :

I LEARNED THIS TODAY :

A PRAYER ON MY HEART TODAY :

MY HIGHLIGHTS OF THE DAY :

Record my misery; list my tears on your scroll— are they not in your record?
Psalm 56:8

TODAY I AM GRATEFUL FOR : _____
_____
_____
_____
_____

KINDNESS I SHARED TODAY : _____
_____
_____
_____
_____

I NEED TO LET GO OF THIS : _____
_____
_____
_____
_____

I LEARNED THIS TODAY : _____
_____
_____
_____
_____

A PRAYER ON MY HEART TODAY : _____
_____
_____
_____
_____

MY HIGHLIGHTS OF THE DAY : _____
_____
_____
_____
_____
_____
_____

Be strong and courageous. Do not be afraid; do not be discouraged,
for the Lord your God will be with you wherever you go.
Joshua 1:9

TODAY I AM GRATEFUL FOR :

KINDNESS I SHARED TODAY :

I NEED TO LET GO OF THIS :

I LEARNED THIS TODAY :

A PRAYER ON MY HEART TODAY :

MY HIGHLIGHTS OF THE DAY :

He will not let your foot slip— he who watches over you will not slumber.
Psalm 121:3

TODAY I AM GRATEFUL FOR : _____

_____

_____

_____

_____

KINDNESS I SHARED TODAY : _____

_____

_____

_____

I NEED TO LET GO OF THIS : _____

_____

_____

_____

I LEARNED THIS TODAY : _____

_____

_____

_____

A PRAYER ON MY HEART TODAY : _____

_____

_____

_____

MY HIGHLIGHTS OF THE DAY : _____

_____

_____

_____

_____

_____

Create in me a pure heart, O God, and
renew a steadfast spirit within me.
Psalm 51:10

TODAY I AM GRATEFUL FOR : _____

_____

_____

_____

_____

KINDNESS I SHARED TODAY : _____

_____

_____

_____

_____

I NEED TO LET GO OF THIS : _____

_____

_____

_____

_____

I LEARNED THIS TODAY : _____

_____

_____

_____

_____

A PRAYER ON MY HEART TODAY : _____

_____

_____

_____

MY HIGHLIGHTS OF THE DAY : _____

_____

_____

_____

_____

_____

Forgive as the Lord forgave you.
Colossians 3:13

TODAY I AM GRATEFUL FOR : _____

_____

_____

_____

_____

KINDNESS I SHARED TODAY : _____

_____

_____

_____

_____

I NEED TO LET GO OF THIS : _____

_____

_____

_____

_____

I LEARNED THIS TODAY : _____

_____

_____

_____

_____

A PRAYER ON MY HEART TODAY : _____

_____

_____

_____

_____

MY HIGHLIGHTS OF THE DAY : _____

_____

_____

_____

_____

Do everything in love.
1 Corinthians 16:14

TODAY I AM GRATEFUL FOR : _____

_____

_____

_____

_____

KINDNESS I SHARED TODAY : _____

_____

_____

_____

_____

I NEED TO LET GO OF THIS : _____

_____

_____

_____

_____

I LEARNED THIS TODAY : _____

_____

_____

_____

_____

A PRAYER ON MY HEART TODAY : _____

_____

_____

_____

MY HIGHLIGHTS OF THE DAY : _____

_____

_____

_____

_____

You are the light of the world.
Matthew 5:14

TODAY I AM GRATEFUL FOR : _____

_____

_____

_____

_____

KINDNESS I SHARED TODAY : _____

_____

_____

_____

_____

I NEED TO LET GO OF THIS : _____

_____

_____

_____

_____

I LEARNED THIS TODAY : _____

_____

_____

_____

_____

A PRAYER ON MY HEART TODAY : _____

_____

_____

_____

_____

MY HIGHLIGHTS OF THE DAY : _____

_____

_____

_____

_____

_____

When you walk through the fire, you will not be burned.
Isaiah 43:2

TODAY I AM GRATEFUL FOR : _____

_____

_____

_____

_____

KINDNESS I SHARED TODAY : _____

_____

_____

_____

_____

I NEED TO LET GO OF THIS : _____

_____

_____

_____

_____

I LEARNED THIS TODAY : _____

_____

_____

_____

_____

A PRAYER ON MY HEART TODAY : _____

_____

_____

_____

MY HIGHLIGHTS OF THE DAY : _____

_____

_____

_____

_____

Be joyful in hope, patient in affliction, faithful in prayer.
Romans 12:12

TODAY I AM GRATEFUL FOR : _____

_____

_____

_____

_____

KINDNESS I SHARED TODAY : _____

_____

_____

_____

_____

I NEED TO LET GO OF THIS : _____

_____

_____

_____

_____

I LEARNED THIS TODAY : _____

_____

_____

_____

_____

A PRAYER ON MY HEART TODAY : _____

_____

_____

_____

_____

MY HIGHLIGHTS OF THE DAY : _____

_____

_____

_____

_____

Clothe yourselves with compassion, kindness,
humility, gentleness and patience.
Colossians 3:12

TODAY I AM GRATEFUL FOR : _____

_____

_____

_____

_____

KINDNESS I SHARED TODAY : _____

_____

_____

_____

_____

I NEED TO LET GO OF THIS : _____

_____

_____

_____

_____

I LEARNED THIS TODAY : _____

_____

_____

_____

_____

A PRAYER ON MY HEART TODAY : _____

_____

_____

_____

_____

MY HIGHLIGHTS OF THE DAY : _____

_____

_____

_____

_____

You also must be ready, because the Son of Man will
come at an hour when you do not expect him.
Luke 12:40

TODAY I AM GRATEFUL FOR : _____

_____

_____

_____

_____

KINDNESS I SHARED TODAY : _____

_____

_____

_____

_____

I NEED TO LET GO OF THIS : _____

_____

_____

_____

_____

I LEARNED THIS TODAY : _____

_____

_____

_____

_____

A PRAYER ON MY HEART TODAY : _____

_____

_____

_____

_____

MY HIGHLIGHTS OF THE DAY : _____

_____

_____

_____

_____

DAY 50 | *Halfway Point*

You are moving along through this journal nicely, and have officially reached the halfway point in your gratitude journey. I'm so happy for you, and hope you're already feeling encouraged! What do you think of this process thus far? Have you noticed a change in your natural thought patterns and focus? Are you more easily able to see the good around you? And are you enjoying how this journal has become part of your routine? If you're feeling any hesitation or doubt about whether gratitude journaling is making a difference, remember that sometimes when we try something new for the first time, it can take a little while to notice the change it's making in our lives. Give it time.

Take a minute to write down your thoughts about how you feel about your gratitude journey so far.

When you're done, flip back through some of your previous entries up to this point and reflect on your current growth.

As water reflects the face, so one's life reflects the heart.
Proverbs 27:19

TODAY I AM GRATEFUL FOR : _____
_____
_____
_____
_____

KINDNESS I SHARED TODAY : _____
_____
_____
_____
_____

I NEED TO LET GO OF THIS : _____
_____
_____
_____
_____

I LEARNED THIS TODAY : _____
_____
_____
_____
_____

A PRAYER ON MY HEART TODAY : _____
_____
_____
_____

MY HIGHLIGHTS OF THE DAY : _____
_____
_____
_____
_____
_____

As for me, I will always have hope; I will praise you more and more.
Psalm 71:14

TODAY I AM GRATEFUL FOR : _____
_____
_____
_____
_____

KINDNESS I SHARED TODAY : _____
_____
_____
_____
_____

I NEED TO LET GO OF THIS : _____
_____
_____
_____
_____

I LEARNED THIS TODAY : _____
_____
_____
_____

A PRAYER ON MY HEART TODAY : _____
_____
_____
_____
_____

MY HIGHLIGHTS OF THE DAY : _____
_____
_____
_____
_____

*Love does not delight in evil but rejoices with the truth. It always
protects, always trusts, always hopes, always perseveres.
1 Corinthians 13:6-7*

TODAY I AM GRATEFUL FOR : _____

_____

_____

_____

_____

KINDNESS I SHARED TODAY : _____

_____

_____

_____

_____

I NEED TO LET GO OF THIS : _____

_____

_____

_____

_____

I LEARNED THIS TODAY : _____

_____

_____

_____

_____

A PRAYER ON MY HEART TODAY : _____

_____

_____

_____

MY HIGHLIGHTS OF THE DAY : _____

_____

_____

_____

_____

*See what great love the Father has lavished on us, that we should be
called children of God! And that is what we are! The reason the world
does not know us is that it did not know him.*
1 John 3:1

TODAY I AM GRATEFUL FOR : _____

_____
_____
_____

KINDNESS I SHARED TODAY : _____

_____
_____
_____

I NEED TO LET GO OF THIS : _____

_____
_____
_____

I LEARNED THIS TODAY : _____

_____
_____
_____

A PRAYER ON MY HEART TODAY : _____

_____
_____
_____

MY HIGHLIGHTS OF THE DAY : _____

_____
_____
_____
_____

So do not fear, for I am with you; do not be dismayed, for I am your God. I will strengthen you and help you; I will uphold you with my righteous right hand.
Isaiah 41:10

TODAY I AM GRATEFUL FOR : _____

_____

_____

_____

_____

KINDNESS I SHARED TODAY : _____

_____

_____

_____

_____

I NEED TO LET GO OF THIS : _____

_____

_____

_____

_____

I LEARNED THIS TODAY : _____

_____

_____

_____

_____

A PRAYER ON MY HEART TODAY : _____

_____

_____

_____

MY HIGHLIGHTS OF THE DAY : _____

_____

_____

_____

_____

_____

If you believe, you will receive whatever you ask for in prayer.
Matthew 21:22

TODAY I AM GRATEFUL FOR : _____

_____

_____

_____

_____

KINDNESS I SHARED TODAY : _____

_____

_____

_____

_____

I NEED TO LET GO OF THIS : _____

_____

_____

_____

_____

I LEARNED THIS TODAY : _____

_____

_____

_____

_____

A PRAYER ON MY HEART TODAY : _____

_____

_____

_____

_____

MY HIGHLIGHTS OF THE DAY : _____

_____

_____

_____

_____

_____

In all your ways submit to him, and he will make your paths straight.
Proverbs 3:6

TODAY I AM GRATEFUL FOR : _____
_____
_____
_____
_____

KINDNESS I SHARED TODAY : _____
_____
_____
_____
_____

I NEED TO LET GO OF THIS : _____
_____
_____
_____
_____

I LEARNED THIS TODAY : _____
_____
_____
_____
_____

A PRAYER ON MY HEART TODAY : _____
_____
_____
_____
_____

MY HIGHLIGHTS OF THE DAY : _____
_____
_____
_____
_____

With man this is impossible, but with God all things are possible.
Matthew 19:26

TODAY I AM GRATEFUL FOR : _____

_____

_____

_____

_____

KINDNESS I SHARED TODAY : _____

_____

_____

_____

_____

I NEED TO LET GO OF THIS : _____

_____

_____

_____

_____

I LEARNED THIS TODAY : _____

_____

_____

_____

_____

A PRAYER ON MY HEART TODAY : _____

_____

_____

_____

MY HIGHLIGHTS OF THE DAY : _____

_____

_____

_____

_____

_____

*Therefore do not worry about tomorrow, for tomorrow will
worry about itself. Each day has enough trouble of its own.
Matthew 6:34*

TODAY I AM GRATEFUL FOR : _____

_____

_____

_____

_____

KINDNESS I SHARED TODAY : _____

_____

_____

_____

_____

I NEED TO LET GO OF THIS : _____

_____

_____

_____

_____

I LEARNED THIS TODAY : _____

_____

_____

_____

_____

A PRAYER ON MY HEART TODAY : _____

_____

_____

_____

MY HIGHLIGHTS OF THE DAY : _____

_____

_____

_____

_____

Cast all your anxiety on him because he cares for you.
1 Peter 5:7

TODAY I AM GRATEFUL FOR : _____

_____

_____

_____

_____

KINDNESS I SHARED TODAY : _____

_____

_____

_____

_____

I NEED TO LET GO OF THIS : _____

_____

_____

_____

_____

I LEARNED THIS TODAY : _____

_____

_____

_____

_____

A PRAYER ON MY HEART TODAY : _____

_____

_____

_____

_____

MY HIGHLIGHTS OF THE DAY : _____

_____

_____

_____

_____

_____

Love never fails.
1 Corinthians 13:8

TODAY I AM GRATEFUL FOR : _____

_____

_____

_____

_____

KINDNESS I SHARED TODAY : _____

_____

_____

_____

_____

I NEED TO LET GO OF THIS : _____

_____

_____

_____

_____

I LEARNED THIS TODAY : _____

_____

_____

_____

_____

A PRAYER ON MY HEART TODAY : _____

_____

_____

_____

MY HIGHLIGHTS OF THE DAY : _____

_____

_____

_____

_____

Be devoted to one another in love.
Honor one another above yourselves.
Romans 12:10

TODAY I AM GRATEFUL FOR : _____

_____

_____

_____

_____

KINDNESS I SHARED TODAY : _____

_____

_____

_____

_____

I NEED TO LET GO OF THIS : _____

_____

_____

_____

_____

I LEARNED THIS TODAY : _____

_____

_____

_____

_____

A PRAYER ON MY HEART TODAY : _____

_____

_____

_____

_____

MY HIGHLIGHTS OF THE DAY : _____

_____

_____

_____

_____

But seek first his kingdom and his righteousness,
and all these things will be given to you as well.
Matthew 6:33

TODAY I AM GRATEFUL FOR : _____

_____

_____

_____

_____

KINDNESS I SHARED TODAY : _____

_____

_____

_____

_____

I NEED TO LET GO OF THIS : _____

_____

_____

_____

_____

I LEARNED THIS TODAY : _____

_____

_____

_____

_____

A PRAYER ON MY HEART TODAY : _____

_____

_____

_____

MY HIGHLIGHTS OF THE DAY : _____

_____

_____

_____

Lord, you alone are my portion and my cup; you make my lot secure.
Psalm 16:5

TODAY I AM GRATEFUL FOR : _____

_____

_____

_____

_____

KINDNESS I SHARED TODAY : _____

_____

_____

_____

_____

I NEED TO LET GO OF THIS : _____

_____

_____

_____

_____

I LEARNED THIS TODAY : _____

_____

_____

_____

_____

A PRAYER ON MY HEART TODAY : _____

_____

_____

_____

_____

MY HIGHLIGHTS OF THE DAY : _____

_____

_____

_____

_____

For God so loved the world that he gave his one and only Son, that
whoever believes in him shall not perish but have eternal life.
John 3:16

TODAY I AM GRATEFUL FOR :

KINDNESS I SHARED TODAY :

I NEED TO LET GO OF THIS :

I LEARNED THIS TODAY :

A PRAYER ON MY HEART TODAY :

MY HIGHLIGHTS OF THE DAY :

Jesus Christ is the same yesterday and today and forever.
Hebrews 13:8

TODAY I AM GRATEFUL FOR :

KINDNESS I SHARED TODAY :

I NEED TO LET GO OF THIS :

I LEARNED THIS TODAY :

A PRAYER ON MY HEART TODAY :

MY HIGHLIGHTS OF THE DAY :

This is the confidence we have in approaching God: that
if we ask anything according to his will, he hears us.
1 John 5:14

TODAY I AM GRATEFUL FOR : _____

_____

_____

_____

_____

KINDNESS I SHARED TODAY : _____

_____

_____

_____

_____

I NEED TO LET GO OF THIS : _____

_____

_____

_____

_____

I LEARNED THIS TODAY : _____

_____

_____

_____

_____

A PRAYER ON MY HEART TODAY : _____

_____

_____

_____

MY HIGHLIGHTS OF THE DAY : _____

_____

_____

_____

_____

"For I know the plans I have for you," declares the Lord, "plans to prosper
you and not to harm you, plans to give you hope and a future.
Jeremiah 29:11

TODAY I AM GRATEFUL FOR : _____

_____

_____

_____

_____

KINDNESS I SHARED TODAY : _____

_____

_____

_____

_____

I NEED TO LET GO OF THIS : _____

_____

_____

_____

_____

I LEARNED THIS TODAY : _____

_____

_____

_____

A PRAYER ON MY HEART TODAY : _____

_____

_____

_____

MY HIGHLIGHTS OF THE DAY : _____

_____

_____

_____

_____

A generous person will prosper; whoever refreshes others will be refreshed.
Proverbs 11:25

TODAY I AM GRATEFUL FOR : _____

_____

_____

_____

_____

KINDNESS I SHARED TODAY : _____

_____

_____

_____

_____

I NEED TO LET GO OF THIS : _____

_____

_____

_____

_____

I LEARNED THIS TODAY : _____

_____

_____

_____

_____

A PRAYER ON MY HEART TODAY : _____

_____

_____

_____

MY HIGHLIGHTS OF THE DAY : _____

_____

_____

_____

_____

Let love and faithfulness never leave you; bind them around
your neck, write them on the tablet of your heart.
Proverbs 3:3

TODAY I AM GRATEFUL FOR : _____

_____

_____

_____

_____

KINDNESS I SHARED TODAY : _____

_____

_____

_____

_____

I NEED TO LET GO OF THIS : _____

_____

_____

_____

_____

I LEARNED THIS TODAY : _____

_____

_____

_____

_____

A PRAYER ON MY HEART TODAY : _____

_____

_____

_____

_____

MY HIGHLIGHTS OF THE DAY : _____

_____

_____

_____

_____

I long to see you so that I may impart to you some
spiritual gift to make you strong— that is, that you and I
may be mutually encouraged by each other's faith.
Romans 1:11-12

TODAY I AM GRATEFUL FOR : _____

_____

_____

_____

_____

KINDNESS I SHARED TODAY : _____

_____

_____

_____

_____

I NEED TO LET GO OF THIS : _____

_____

_____

_____

_____

I LEARNED THIS TODAY : _____

_____

_____

_____

_____

A PRAYER ON MY HEART TODAY : _____

_____

_____

_____

_____

MY HIGHLIGHTS OF THE DAY : _____

_____

_____

_____

_____

For where two or three gather in my name, there am I with them.
Matthew 18:20

TODAY I AM GRATEFUL FOR : _____

_____

_____

_____

_____

KINDNESS I SHARED TODAY : _____

_____

_____

_____

_____

I NEED TO LET GO OF THIS : _____

_____

_____

_____

_____

I LEARNED THIS TODAY : _____

_____

_____

_____

_____

A PRAYER ON MY HEART TODAY : _____

_____

_____

_____

_____

MY HIGHLIGHTS OF THE DAY : _____

_____

_____

_____

_____

_____

For where your treasure is, there your heart will be also.
Matthew 6:21

TODAY I AM GRATEFUL FOR :

KINDNESS I SHARED TODAY :

I NEED TO LET GO OF THIS :

I LEARNED THIS TODAY :

A PRAYER ON MY HEART TODAY :

MY HIGHLIGHTS OF THE DAY :

I praise you because I am fearfully and wonderfully made,
your works are wonderful, I know that full well.
Psalm 139: 14

TODAY I AM GRATEFUL FOR :

KINDNESS I SHARED TODAY :

I NEED TO LET GO OF THIS :

I LEARNED THIS TODAY :

A PRAYER ON MY HEART TODAY :

MY HIGHLIGHTS OF THE DAY :

In the beginning God created...
Genesis 1:1

TODAY I AM GRATEFUL FOR : _____
_____
_____
_____
_____

KINDNESS I SHARED TODAY : _____
_____
_____
_____
_____

I NEED TO LET GO OF THIS : _____
_____
_____
_____
_____

I LEARNED THIS TODAY : _____
_____
_____
_____
_____

A PRAYER ON MY HEART TODAY : _____
_____
_____
_____
_____

MY HIGHLIGHTS OF THE DAY : _____
_____
_____
_____
_____
_____

Before I formed you in the womb I knew you,
before you were born I set you apart.
Jeremiah 1:5

TODAY I AM GRATEFUL FOR :

KINDNESS I SHARED TODAY :

I NEED TO LET GO OF THIS :

I LEARNED THIS TODAY :

A PRAYER ON MY HEART TODAY :

MY HIGHLIGHTS OF THE DAY :

Rise up; this matter is in your hands. We will
support you, so take courage and do it.
Ezra 10:4

TODAY I AM GRATEFUL FOR :

KINDNESS I SHARED TODAY :

I NEED TO LET GO OF THIS :

I LEARNED THIS TODAY :

A PRAYER ON MY HEART TODAY :

MY HIGHLIGHTS OF THE DAY :

If the world hates you, keep in mind that it hated me first.
John 15:18

TODAY I AM GRATEFUL FOR : _____

_____

_____

_____

_____

KINDNESS I SHARED TODAY : _____

_____

_____

_____

I NEED TO LET GO OF THIS : _____

_____

_____

_____

I LEARNED THIS TODAY : _____

_____

_____

_____

A PRAYER ON MY HEART TODAY : _____

_____

_____

_____

MY HIGHLIGHTS OF THE DAY : _____

_____

_____

_____

_____

The grass withers and the flowers fall, but the word of our God endures forever.
Isaiah 40:8

TODAY I AM GRATEFUL FOR :

KINDNESS I SHARED TODAY :

I NEED TO LET GO OF THIS :

I LEARNED THIS TODAY :

A PRAYER ON MY HEART TODAY :

MY HIGHLIGHTS OF THE DAY :

All Scripture is God-breathed and is useful for teaching, rebuking,
correcting and training in righteousness, so that the servant of God
may be thoroughly equipped for every good work.
2 Timothy 3:16-17

TODAY I AM GRATEFUL FOR : _____

_____

_____

_____

KINDNESS I SHARED TODAY : _____

_____

_____

_____

I NEED TO LET GO OF THIS : _____

_____

_____

_____

I LEARNED THIS TODAY : _____

_____

_____

_____

A PRAYER ON MY HEART TODAY : _____

_____

_____

_____

MY HIGHLIGHTS OF THE DAY : _____

_____

_____

_____

*Be kind and compassionate to one another, forgiving
each other, just as in Christ God forgave you.*
Ephesians 4:32

TODAY I AM GRATEFUL FOR :

KINDNESS I SHARED TODAY :

I NEED TO LET GO OF THIS :

I LEARNED THIS TODAY :

A PRAYER ON MY HEART TODAY :

MY HIGHLIGHTS OF THE DAY :

In all this you greatly rejoice, though now for a little while
you may have had to suffer grief in all kinds of trials.
1 Peter 1:6

TODAY I AM GRATEFUL FOR : _____

_____

_____

_____

_____

KINDNESS I SHARED TODAY : _____

_____

_____

_____

_____

I NEED TO LET GO OF THIS : _____

_____

_____

_____

_____

I LEARNED THIS TODAY : _____

_____

_____

_____

_____

A PRAYER ON MY HEART TODAY : _____

_____

_____

_____

_____

MY HIGHLIGHTS OF THE DAY : _____

_____

_____

_____

_____

_____

_____

Our struggle is not against flesh and blood, but against the rulers,
against the authorities, against the powers of this dark world and
against the spiritual forces of evil in the heavenly realms.
Ephesians 6:12

TODAY I AM GRATEFUL FOR : _____

_____

_____

_____

_____

KINDNESS I SHARED TODAY : _____

_____

_____

_____

_____

I NEED TO LET GO OF THIS : _____

_____

_____

_____

_____

I LEARNED THIS TODAY : _____

_____

_____

_____

_____

A PRAYER ON MY HEART TODAY : _____

_____

_____

_____

MY HIGHLIGHTS OF THE DAY : _____

_____

_____

_____

_____

Everyone who wants to live a godly life in Christ Jesus will be persecuted.
2 Timothy 3:12

TODAY I AM GRATEFUL FOR : _____

_____

_____

_____

_____

KINDNESS I SHARED TODAY : _____

_____

_____

_____

_____

I NEED TO LET GO OF THIS : _____

_____

_____

_____

_____

I LEARNED THIS TODAY : _____

_____

_____

_____

_____

A PRAYER ON MY HEART TODAY : _____

_____

_____

_____

MY HIGHLIGHTS OF THE DAY : _____

_____

_____

_____

_____

Fear God and keep his commandments, for this is the duty of all mankind.
Ecclesiastes 12:13

TODAY I AM GRATEFUL FOR :

KINDNESS I SHARED TODAY :

I NEED TO LET GO OF THIS :

I LEARNED THIS TODAY :

A PRAYER ON MY HEART TODAY :

MY HIGHLIGHTS OF THE DAY :

*In the same way, the Spirit helps us in our weakness. We do not know what we
ought to pray for, but the Spirit himself intercedes for us through wordless groans.*
Romans 8:26

TODAY I AM GRATEFUL FOR : _____

_____

_____

_____

_____

KINDNESS I SHARED TODAY : _____

_____

_____

_____

_____

I NEED TO LET GO OF THIS : _____

_____

_____

_____

_____

I LEARNED THIS TODAY : _____

_____

_____

_____

_____

A PRAYER ON MY HEART TODAY : _____

_____

_____

_____

_____

MY HIGHLIGHTS OF THE DAY : _____

_____

_____

_____

_____

_____

_____

Love is patient, love is kind. It does not envy, it does not boast, it is not proud.
1 Corinthians 13:4

TODAY I AM GRATEFUL FOR : _____

_____

_____

_____

_____

KINDNESS I SHARED TODAY : _____

_____

_____

_____

_____

I NEED TO LET GO OF THIS : _____

_____

_____

_____

_____

I LEARNED THIS TODAY : _____

_____

_____

_____

A PRAYER ON MY HEART TODAY : _____

_____

_____

_____

MY HIGHLIGHTS OF THE DAY : _____

_____

_____

_____

_____

Those who guard their lips preserve their lives.
Proverbs 13:3

TODAY I AM GRATEFUL FOR : _____

_____

_____

_____

_____

KINDNESS I SHARED TODAY : _____

_____

_____

_____

_____

I NEED TO LET GO OF THIS : _____

_____

_____

_____

_____

I LEARNED THIS TODAY : _____

_____

_____

_____

_____

A PRAYER ON MY HEART TODAY : _____

_____

_____

_____

_____

MY HIGHLIGHTS OF THE DAY : _____

_____

_____

_____

_____

_____

Gracious words are a honeycomb, sweet to the soul and healing to the bones.
Proverbs 16:24

TODAY I AM GRATEFUL FOR :

KINDNESS I SHARED TODAY :

I NEED TO LET GO OF THIS :

I LEARNED THIS TODAY :

A PRAYER ON MY HEART TODAY :

MY HIGHLIGHTS OF THE DAY :

A friend loves at all times.
Proverbs 17:17

TODAY I AM GRATEFUL FOR :

KINDNESS I SHARED TODAY :

I NEED TO LET GO OF THIS :

I LEARNED THIS TODAY :

A PRAYER ON MY HEART TODAY :

MY HIGHLIGHTS OF THE DAY :

The Lord lives! Praise be to my Rock! Exalted be God my Savior!
Psalm 18:46

TODAY I AM GRATEFUL FOR :

KINDNESS I SHARED TODAY :

I NEED TO LET GO OF THIS :

I LEARNED THIS TODAY :

A PRAYER ON MY HEART TODAY :

MY HIGHLIGHTS OF THE DAY :

Dear friends, since God so loved us, we also ought to love one another.
1 John 4:11

TODAY I AM GRATEFUL FOR : _____
_____
_____
_____
_____

KINDNESS I SHARED TODAY : _____
_____
_____
_____
_____

I NEED TO LET GO OF THIS : _____
_____
_____
_____
_____

I LEARNED THIS TODAY : _____
_____
_____
_____
_____

A PRAYER ON MY HEART TODAY : _____
_____
_____
_____
_____

MY HIGHLIGHTS OF THE DAY : _____
_____
_____
_____
_____
_____

How wide and long and high and deep is the love of Christ.
Ephesians 3:18

TODAY I AM GRATEFUL FOR : _____

_____

_____

_____

_____

KINDNESS I SHARED TODAY : _____

_____

_____

_____

_____

I NEED TO LET GO OF THIS : _____

_____

_____

_____

_____

I LEARNED THIS TODAY : _____

_____

_____

_____

_____

A PRAYER ON MY HEART TODAY : _____

_____

_____

_____

MY HIGHLIGHTS OF THE DAY : _____

_____

_____

_____

_____

_____

However, if you suffer as a Christian, do not be ashamed,
but praise God that you bear that name.
1 Peter 4:16

TODAY I AM GRATEFUL FOR : _____

_____

_____

_____

_____

KINDNESS I SHARED TODAY : _____

_____

_____

_____

_____

I NEED TO LET GO OF THIS : _____

_____

_____

_____

_____

I LEARNED THIS TODAY : _____

_____

_____

_____

_____

A PRAYER ON MY HEART TODAY : _____

_____

_____

_____

MY HIGHLIGHTS OF THE DAY : _____

_____

_____

_____

_____

And now these three remain: faith, hope and love.
But the greatest of these is love.
1 Corinthians 13:13

TODAY I AM GRATEFUL FOR : _____

_____

_____

_____

_____

KINDNESS I SHARED TODAY : _____

_____

_____

_____

_____

I NEED TO LET GO OF THIS : _____

_____

_____

_____

_____

I LEARNED THIS TODAY : _____

_____

_____

_____

_____

A PRAYER ON MY HEART TODAY : _____

_____

_____

_____

MY HIGHLIGHTS OF THE DAY : _____

_____

_____

_____

_____

The Lord has done it this very day; let us rejoice today and be glad.
Psalm 118:24

TODAY I AM GRATEFUL FOR : _____
_____
_____
_____
_____

KINDNESS I SHARED TODAY : _____
_____
_____
_____
_____

I NEED TO LET GO OF THIS : _____
_____
_____
_____
_____

I LEARNED THIS TODAY : _____
_____
_____
_____
_____

A PRAYER ON MY HEART TODAY : _____
_____
_____
_____
_____

MY HIGHLIGHTS OF THE DAY : _____
_____
_____
_____
_____
_____
_____

Peace I leave with you; my peace I give you. I do not give to you as the world gives. Do not let your hearts be troubled and do not be afraid.
John 14:27

TODAY I AM GRATEFUL FOR : _____

_____

_____

_____

_____

KINDNESS I SHARED TODAY : _____

_____

_____

_____

_____

I NEED TO LET GO OF THIS : _____

_____

_____

_____

_____

I LEARNED THIS TODAY : _____

_____

_____

_____

_____

A PRAYER ON MY HEART TODAY : _____

_____

_____

_____

MY HIGHLIGHTS OF THE DAY : _____

_____

_____

_____

God saw all that he had made, and it was very good.
Genesis 1:31

TODAY I AM GRATEFUL FOR : _____

_____

_____

_____

_____

KINDNESS I SHARED TODAY : _____

_____

_____

_____

_____

I NEED TO LET GO OF THIS : _____

_____

_____

_____

_____

I LEARNED THIS TODAY : _____

_____

_____

_____

_____

A PRAYER ON MY HEART TODAY : _____

_____

_____

_____

_____

MY HIGHLIGHTS OF THE DAY : _____

_____

_____

_____

_____

_____

*But he knows the way that I take; when he
has tested me, I will come forth as gold.*
Job 23:10

TODAY I AM GRATEFUL FOR : _____

_____

_____

_____

_____

KINDNESS I SHARED TODAY : _____

_____

_____

_____

_____

I NEED TO LET GO OF THIS : _____

_____

_____

_____

_____

I LEARNED THIS TODAY : _____

_____

_____

_____

A PRAYER ON MY HEART TODAY : _____

_____

_____

_____

MY HIGHLIGHTS OF THE DAY : _____

_____

_____

_____

_____

*Therefore, if anyone is in Christ, the new creation
has come: The old has gone, the new is here!*
2 Corinthians 5:17

TODAY I AM GRATEFUL FOR : _____

_____

_____

_____

_____

KINDNESS I SHARED TODAY : _____

_____

_____

_____

_____

I NEED TO LET GO OF THIS : _____

_____

_____

_____

_____

I LEARNED THIS TODAY : _____

_____

_____

_____

_____

A PRAYER ON MY HEART TODAY : _____

_____

_____

_____

_____

MY HIGHLIGHTS OF THE DAY : _____

_____

_____

_____

_____

DAY 100 | *Wrap-Up*

You made it! How was it? Do you feel different? Changed? Perhaps more easily able to see the good around you despite the trials that lay at your feet? Use the blank pages that follow to pen your thoughts surrounding your current state of mind and heart.

After you write down your thoughts, go back and read the entry for Day One. How does it feel to see where you were? How does it feel to reflect on where you are now? Whatever you feel today, honor the fact that you committed yourself to this gratitude practice. Each day is different, and they won't always be easy, but the fact that you've gifted a few minutes to yourself each day shows you are steadfast in your effort to grow.

You're amazing, and I'm proud of you for being intentional with your time and doing the daily heart work through this season! I pray this journal lifted you in a way that makes you feel lighter and brighter for the days ahead.

If you enjoyed this practice and aren't ready to see it end, grab another copy and start all over. Continue to let your heart journey unfold!

Again, congratulations on showing up for 100 days of *More Than Gratitude!*

YOUR STORIES ARE WORTH TELLING

We believe this in our core, which is why we're creating the heirloom books that we do. We believe in quality materials, timeless design, and a whole lot of heart. We invite you to visit our website to dive into any of the books in our current lineup and get a deeper look at the contents, purpose of the book, who it's for, and what makes each one special.

WWW.KORIEHEROLD.COM
for more information

OTHER BOOKS BY KORIE HEROLD

***GROWING YOU : A KEEPSAKE PREGNANCY JOURNAL AND MEMORY BOOK FOR MOM
& BABY*** - *Growing You* is a place to celebrate and chronicle your pregnancy journey,
reflecting on the growth, anticipation, and memories that you want to hold onto as
a mother. This heirloom-quality book is designed with a timeless look and archival
paper so that you can one day pass it along to your child. This journal is perfect to gift
someone early on in their pregnancy.

AS YOU GROW : A MODERN MEMORY BOOK FOR BABY - A modern take on a baby
memory book and journal, *As You Grow* stands out from the crowd of baby books
with its elegant, chic, and timeless design. The gender-neutral artwork with guided
sections provide space for your family to record moments from pregnancy to age five.
It's a book you can interact with now, and look back on for a lifetime. The design
promotes longevity, as this keepsake book is intended to be shared and displayed for
years to come. *As You Grow* is inclusive of every modern family. This book makes a
great gift for a parent at a baby shower.

GROWING UP : A MODERN MEMORY BOOK FOR THE SCHOOL YEARS - *Growing Up* is
a modern memory book for the school years and features gender-neutral artwork and
space to record precious memories from each year of your child's schooling so you can
one day gift to your grown child. The book includes space to record moments for each
grade level from kindergarten through high school.

OUR CHRISTMAS STORY : A MODERN MEMORY BOOK FOR CHRISTMAS - Cherish
your favorite memories by writing down meaningful traditions, remember holiday
celebrations you hosted or attended, record special gifts given or received, save photos
with Santa or annual family Christmas cards, preserve treasured family holiday recipes,
and so much more! This book makes for a thoughtful gift for a bridal shower, wedding
gift, or for a family who loves to celebrate Christmas.

***AROUND OUR TABLE : A MODERN HEIRLOOM RECIPE BOOK TO ORGANIZE AND
PRESERVE YOUR FAMILY'S MOST CHERISHED MEALS*** - Your family's most cherished
meals deserve to be remembered. Preserve all of your favorite recipes, and the
memories associated with them, in this heirloom-quality blank recipe book. The book
includes 7 sections to organize your recipes, blank recipe pages, 20 loose recipe cards,
plastic sleeves to preserve new and old recipes, and a pocket folder in the back for
additional storage.

AS WE GROW : A MODERN MEMORY BOOK FOR MARRIED COUPLES - *As We Grow* is a
place to celebrate and remember the details of your marriage. Record the story of how
you live and love and preserve it in writing—a treasure you can pass to your children
and grandchildren. It's the perfect gift for the newly engaged couple, the newly
married couple, or those who have been married for years!

WHAT PEOPLE ARE SAYING
ABOUT KORIE HEROLD BOOKS

"Korie is an artist at heart but also has an overwhelming sense of legacy to everything she does. Her other books have a way of making you pause, slow down, and memorialize a fleeting season to enjoy later." - Lauren Swann

"When you see how beautiful and detail-oriented her books are, you become a customer for life. Thank you, Korie, for thinking of everything and creating treasures that will be passed down through future generations." - Paige Frey

"The quality is unbelievable and it's such a gorgeous place to preserve all those cherished memories. And it looks beautiful on my shelf next to my other memory books from Korie! … I love the attention to detail Korie includes in her books." - Maria Hilsenbrand

"By far, I think my favorite thing about As You Grow *is that my son will one day be able to cherish this time capsule of sorts. He'll know exactly how he was loved, thought of, and remembered as my sweet little boy."*
- Alyse Morrissey

WWW.KORIEHEROLD.COM